YAO MING

International Basketball Star

Therese Shea

The Tony Stead NONFICTION INDEPENDENT READING COLLECTION

Rosen Classroom Books & Materials™
New York

Published in 2006 by The Rosen Publishing Group, Inc.
29 East 21st Street, New York, NY 10010

First Edition

Editor: Kerri O'Donnell
Designer: Daniel Hosek

Photo Credits: Cover, pp. 9, 17 © Rueters/Corbis; p. 5 © William R. Sallaz/NewSport/Corbis; p. 7 © Gary Caskey/Reuters/Corbis; pp. 11, 15 © AFP/Getty Images; p. 13 © Claro Cortes IV/Reuters/Corbis; p. 19 © Mike Blake/Reuters/Corbis; pp. 21, 22 © Lucy Nicholson/Reuters/Corbis.

Library of Congress Cataloging-in-Publication Data

Shea, Therese.
Yao Ming : international basketball star / Therese Shea.
p. cm. — (The Tony Stead nonfiction independent reading collection)
ISBN 1-4042-5538-9 (pbk.)
1. Yao, Ming, 1980—Juvenile literature. 2. Basketball players—China—Biography—Juvenile literature. I. Title. II. Series.
GV884.Y36S54 2006
796.323'092—dc22

2005003627

Manufactured in the United States of America

CPSIA Compliance Information: Batch #WR412180RC:
For further information contact Rosen Publishing, New York, New York at 1-800-237-9932.

CONTENTS

BORN TO PLAY BASKETBALL

Have you ever heard people say that they were born to do something? This means that they have a special talent. The basketball player Yao Ming has probably heard people say he was born to play basketball. He was a star basketball player in China before he came to the United States to play in the National Basketball **Association** (NBA).

In 2003, Yao Ming was voted Rookie of the Year by the newspaper The Sporting News. *This means he was voted the best new player in the NBA.*

CHINESE NAMES

Yao Ming was born in Shanghai, China, on September 12, 1980. In China, a person's first name is the family name. If your name were Kim Lopez in the United States, it would be Lopez Kim in China. If Yao followed the usual way of doing things in the United States, his name would be Ming Yao. However, most people call him Yao. This is his name in Chinese:

姚明

Yao is 7 feet 6 inches (229 cm) tall! Here he is next to a player named Earl Boykins, who is 5 feet 5 inches (165 cm) tall. ▶

NUGGETS
11
DN

YAO'S FAMILY

Yao's parents were talented basketball players. They are both very tall, but not as tall as Yao. His father's name is Yao Zhi Yuan. He is 6 feet 7 inches (201 cm) tall. His mother's name is Fang Feng Di. She is 6 feet 3 inches (191 cm) tall. They both played **professional** basketball in China. Yao has said that his parents were his best coaches.

Yao's mother, Fang Feng Di, was the captain of the Chinese national team when it won the Asian Championship in 1976. Here she looks at a poster of her son.

GROWING UP QUICKLY

Yao was 4 feet 9 inches (145 cm) tall by the time he was 5 years old. His doctors guessed that he would grow to be over 7 feet (213 cm) tall.

In China, children who seem like they will become good **athletes** are invited to go to a sports school. Because Yao was tall and his parents were basketball players, he was asked to attend the Youth Sports School.

Yao had an illness when he was young. The medicine he took for the illness made him deaf in his left ear.

上海
SHARKS

YAO'S EARLY CAREER

Yao learned to play basketball when he was 9 years old at sports school. When he was 13 years old, he was asked to join the Shanghai Sharks junior team. Because he was so tall, he played in the center position. At his training camp, he practiced 10 hours a day. He could only go home on weekends.

In this picture, Yao (left) plays against his best friend, Liu Wei, in an NBA game. They both played for the Shanghai Sharks. ▶

ROCKETS
11

EXPANDING HIS WORLD

In 1997, Yao left China for the first time to attend a basketball camp in Paris, France. The next year, Yao joined the Shanghai Sharks senior team in the Chinese Basketball Association (CBA). In his first year, he had an **average** of 10 points and 8.3 **rebounds** per game. More importantly, he learned to trust his teammates and to be a team player.

Yao broke his left foot twice in 2 years when he played for Shanghai. He says that he cannot jump as high as he once could.

THE BIG MOVE

In 2002, Yao and the Sharks won their first national **championship**. He averaged 41 points in each of the final games!

Yao decided he wanted to come to the United States and join the National Basketball Association (NBA). Many NBA teams wanted him, including the Houston Rockets, who received the first pick in the **draft** that year. This means Yao was the first player chosen to join the NBA that year.

Yao Ming was the first player from a country other than the United States to be the NBA's number-one draft pick. In this picture, he talks with the coach of the Houston Rockets.

ALL-STAR

Yao worked hard during his first year in the NBA and improved with every game. Sometimes, when players are as tall as Yao, they cannot score points or move quickly. Yao finished the 2002–2003 season averaging 13.5 points, 8.2 rebounds, and 1.7 **blocks** per game. Yao was voted to be an All-Star. This means fans thought he was one of the most talented players in the NBA.

This picture shows Yao playing in the 2004 NBA All-Star Game.

JUST GETTING BETTER

After his first year in the NBA, Yao returned to China. He had promised to continue to play for his country's national team every year after the NBA season was over.

In his second year in the NBA, Yao improved. He averaged 17.5 points, 9 rebounds, and 1.9 blocks per game. Yao was again chosen as an All-Star. He even helped the Houston Rockets get to the **playoffs**.

Yao has learned a lot from playing against famous basketball player Shaquille O'Neill, shown on the left.

INTERNATIONAL STAR

When he was young, Yao wanted to find adventure all over the world. He has done this through basketball. In 2004, he even led the Chinese national team to the **Olympics** in Athens, Greece. Wherever he goes, Yao finds many new fans and friends. These fans and friends have at least two things in common. They love basketball, and they love its rising star, Yao Ming.

Here, Yao carries China's flag at the 2004 Olympics.

GLOSSARY

association (uh-soh-see-AY-shun) A group of people with a common interest.

athlete (ATH-leet) A person who trains for and is skilled in a sport.

average (AA-vrij) A number that reflects the middle value of a set of numbers.

block (BLAHK) In basketball, the act of stopping the ball from entering the basket.

championship (CHAM-pea-uhn-ship) A contest held to decide first place.

draft (DRAFT) A system of choosing new players for sports teams.

Olympics (uh-LIM-piks) Contests of sports skills in which people from all over the world take part.

playoffs (PLAY-offs) A series of games played after the regular season to decide a championship.

professional (pruh-FEH-shuh-nuhl) Played by people who are paid to take part.

rebound (REE-bownd) The act of gaining control of the basketball after a missed shot.

INDEX

WEB SITES

Due to the changing nature of Internet links, the Rosen Publishing Group, Inc., has developed an online list of Web sites related to the subject of this book. This site is updated regularly. Please use this link to access the list:

http://www.rcbmlinks.com/tsirc/yaoming/